THIS BOOK IS FOR

BORN

LOTS OF LOVE
FORVER & ALWAYS

38230409R00085

Made in the USA
Lexington, KY
06 May 2019